The World's Terriblesssst Jokes Book

The Stress Buster Book Of 50 Irritating Yet Oddly Satisfying Jokes For Kids 6-8 & 9-12 And For The Kids @ Heart

(Now, that laugh is annoying, stop, have some dee-sen-see!)

A truckload of awesome, rib tickling, irritating and roll-on-the-floor-laffing jokes every kid should tell his friends and see them mad (or see them roll on the floor).

(Note From The Author's Teacher: "Terriblessst" is the most terrible grammatical and spelling error in the world. And deesensee, really? You can send the author to detention if you like.)

Bam TulOOkey

This Book Belongs To:

To mom & dad

1

It has wings but it can't fly...
But it smells like an ice cream.
What is it?

2

Silly Billy's home was robbed.
They took away everything
but the TV.
Why?

1 Answer

A fly that fell into
vanilla essence.

2 Answer

Because Silly Billy
was watching TV, silly.

3

If you call your mother, 'mom',
then what should you be calling
your mother's elder sis and
younger sis?

4

What looks exactly like a lizard,
is on the wall too,
but never moves?

Minimom & Maximom

4 Answer

A lizard's picture on the wall.
(He died last month)

5

If you look at it, it looks back at you. If you laugh out too loud, it cries. And if you eat, it drowns in water. What's is it?

6

Once upon a time, one angry ant threw an elephant into a flowing river. But the elephant came out without getting wet. How?

5 Answer

A mirror, an infant and a platter (When did I say I was talking about the same thing?)

6 Answer

It was a waterproof elephant.

7

What should you do so that you would not get hurt even if you jump from the sky without a parachute?

8

What should your dad's email password be if your mother should never get it?

7 Answer

1. Die
2. Be reborn as an ant
3. Get into a flight
4. Jump

8 Answer

Silence

9

Watching a red ant jump into the red sea, a lizard jumped into a muddy puddle. Why?

10

What is the opposite of electricity?

Red and red – matching – matching
Brown and brown – matching
matching

Don't-elect plant village
Confused?
Elect-tri-city

11

Why did the chicken drink water?

12

Detective elephant painted himself white when he sneaked into the notorious ant's home. Why?

11 Answer

Because it is not possible to eat water

12 Answer

So that he'd not get noticed when he hides in the sugar can

13

You find it in the sky.
But it is also on land.
It is easily visible in the dark.
And some people love to eat it.
What is it?

14

You throw a ball up into the air
but it does not come down.
What does it mean?

13 Answer

Ship! I forgot the answer
Hee hee

14 Answer

It means that the guy on the
first floor balcony is a champ in
catching the ball.

15

Once, an ant was riding a motorbike and on the way, she saw her husband asking for a lift. The ant did not stop. Why?

16

This is an animal with big ears and weighs 2,700 kgs. If you see it here now, in a minute it would be found 63 miles away. What's it?

15 Answer

Because the ant was pregnant. Triple riding is an offence.

16 Answer

An elephant sitting on the roof of a bullet train that's speeding at 63 miles a minute.

17

Why did everybody who returned rich from Africa build a new home?

18

Who gets depressed each night when you sleep?

17 Answer

Because it's not possible to build an old home.

18 Answer

Your pillow

19

What's it that never gets dirty, how much ever you drag it through dirt?

20

You know why dogs wag their tails. But why did dinosaurs wag their tails?

19 Answer

Your shadow

20 Answer

Because the tails can't wag dinosaurs

21

How could we get the power
to walk on water?

22

What has three legs
and when you use it,
you'd see a doctor?

21 Answer

By turning that water into ice

22 Answer

A broken chair

23

What has six legs
and sings well?

24

What is white and sits on the
television?

A band of three singers

A fly in a white frock

25

What is black, white, red, black, white red?

26

What sits on a tree and goes 'hrrrrr... hrrrr'?

25 Answer

A zebra that got slapped by the school bully

26 Answer

A cuckoo with a soar throat

27

A baby snake went out to buy toffees, realized that she forgot the money at home and then promptly died. Why?

28

What is beautiful, green in color and has two wheels?

27 Answer

Because she bit her tongue

28 Answer

The painting of a meadow with a bicycle parked in it

29

What is round, white and rolls
up the mountain slope?

30

What did the cannibal have
when he visited McDonalds?

A snowy boulder that got bored of rolling down slopes

A crew member

31

An ant called Just, asked for bread. The cash was 25cents short. But the baker elephant gave the ant two packs of bread. Why?

32

What is almost round, red on the outside and brown inside, and is eaten by vegetarians and non-vegetarians alike?

31 Answer

Just like that

32 Answer

A potato wearing a red jacket

33

What has a little trunk and flies in the air?

34

What gets dirty after taking a shower?

A honey bee in an elephant's disguise

The bathroom

35

What looks exactly like a pigeon
but does not fly?
No, it's not toy.

36

What's yellow in color and sings?

35 Answer

A terribly obese pigeon walking to the gym

36 Answer

A mango (the 'sings' part was just to confuse you... hee hee)
Okay, fine! The real answer is... A Yellow Singer

37

What has a round head, a little tail, weighs tons and keeps moving around?

38

What's the difference between a fly and an elephant?

An elephant on a motorbike wearing a helmet

The fly can sit on the elephant

39

One little lamb jumped the fence and escaped when her friend kept staring at her from inside. Just then someone sang, "Smack that..." Who did?

40

It happened, that once an ant jumped into a well and lots of water splashed out. But when the elephant jumped into the well, not a drop came out. Why?

Akon. Lambs can't sing

The well that the elephant jumped, had no water. When did I say they jumped into the same well?

41

An ant and an elephant were riding a bike. Unfortunately, there was an accident and the ant died. But the elephant did not die. Why?

42

Silly Billy heard the captain announce that all the engines of the flight failed. He instantly jumped out of the flight. But he didn't die. Why?

41 Answer

Because the elephant was already dead. The ant was riding his friendly ghost

42 Answer

Because the plane didn't take off yet

43

A shopkeeper sold a talking elephant to Silly Billy. He said the elephant will answer whatever you ask. But reaching home the elephant did not answer any questions. Why?

44

My brother and I were relaxing on easy chairs on a Sunday afternoon. I saw one big baboon entering the house. But my brother who was next to me, couldn't see it. Why?

43 Answer

The elephant was deaf

44 Answer

How can *he* see what's happening in *my* dream?

45

When a cobra bit little Sammy, nothing happened to him. Why?

46

One day, Mr. Pull took a leak in the restroom, while he spoke on his mobile. And then, the urine followed him everywhere he went. Why?

45 Answer

Because little Sammy was a cobra too. Now, if that's his name, what can I do 'bout it?

46 Answer

Because Mr. Pull was talking on a Nokia. You know, Nokia - Connects pee, Pull

47

A chicken and a dog were watching videos on YouTube, sitting in a garden. It suddenly rained heavily. The chicken sneezed but the dog did not. Why?

48

What eats dirt and is found on top of a skyscraper?

Because the dog was a toy, not a
real one

48 Answer

A vacuum cleaner
vexed with life

49

A chicken and a dog were watching videos on YouTube again, in the garden. It suddenly rained heavily. The chicken sneezed but the dog didn't. Why? (The dog was real this time)

50

A small medium at large. What does that mean?

49 Answer

Because the rain was not real. It was in the YouTube video.

50 Answer

A very short fortune teller who broke out of prison

51

A chicken and a dog were watching videos in a garden, when it rained heavily. The chicken sneezed but the dog didn't. Why? (This time, dog was real and so was the rain)

51 Answer

No idea. Why don't you call up the dog and ask, huh?

My number:

Thanks For Owning This Book

Visit
WWW.Tulookey.com
for more syooprrr books and
surprise goodies.

About the author

Bam Tulookey is a dreamer and a misfit.

Early in life, everybody in his huge joint family said he was immensely talented. He truly believed he was a hero. But when he joined the school, nobody cared a lizard's dropping. He became one of the most thrashed and punished guys at school.

But when in middle school, Bam Tulookey realized that he was not actually a moron but really a misfit. With that, sprang out the rebel from inside him. And then, he executed lots of mischief and relaxed into a happy self-acceptance.

In the later years, he kicked double MBA degrees, a corporate career and turned a music composer, actor, voice artist, radio jock, behavioral trainer and finally a novelist.

For more visit WWW.Tulookey.com